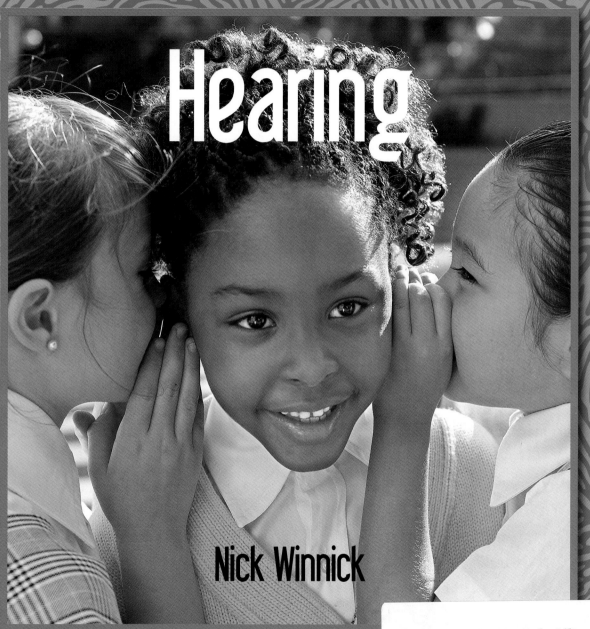

Hearing

Nick Winnick

Published by Weigl Publishers Inc.
350 5th Avenue, Suite 3304, PMB 6G
New York, NY 10118-0069
Website: www.weigl.com

Library of Congress Cataloging-in-Publication Data

Winnick, Nick.
 Hearing / Nick Winnick.
     p. cm. -- (World of wonder)
 Includes index.
 ISBN 978-1-60596-054-8 (hard cover : alk. paper) -- ISBN 978-1-60596-055-5 (soft cover : alk. paper)
 1. Hearing--Juvenile literature. 2. Sound--Juvenile literature. I. Title.
 QP462.2.W56 2010
 612.8'5--dc22

                          2009001961

Printed in China
1 2 3 4 5 6 7 8 9 0 13 12 11 10 09

Editor: Heather C. Hudak
Design and Layout: Terry Paulhus

All of the Internet URLs given in the book were valid at the time of publication. However, due to the dynamic nature of the Internet, some addresses may have changed, or sites may have ceased to exist since publication. While the author and publisher regret any inconvenience this may cause readers, no responsibility for any such changes can be accepted by either the author or the publisher.

Every reasonable effort has been made to trace ownership and to obtain permission to reprint copyright material. The publishers would be pleased to have any errors or omissions brought to their attention so that they may be corrected in subsequent printings.

Weigl acknowledges Getty Images as its primary image supplier for this title.

CONTENTS

What is Hearing?

How do you know when your friend is talking or a dog is barking? Your ears tell you so. Sounds are made up of tiny **pulses** of air. Our ears send these pulses to the brain.

Hearing is one of the **senses**. It helps us learn about our surroundings. Walk outside, and listen closely. What sounds do you hear?

Crickets do not have ears. They have patches of skin on their legs that sense sound.

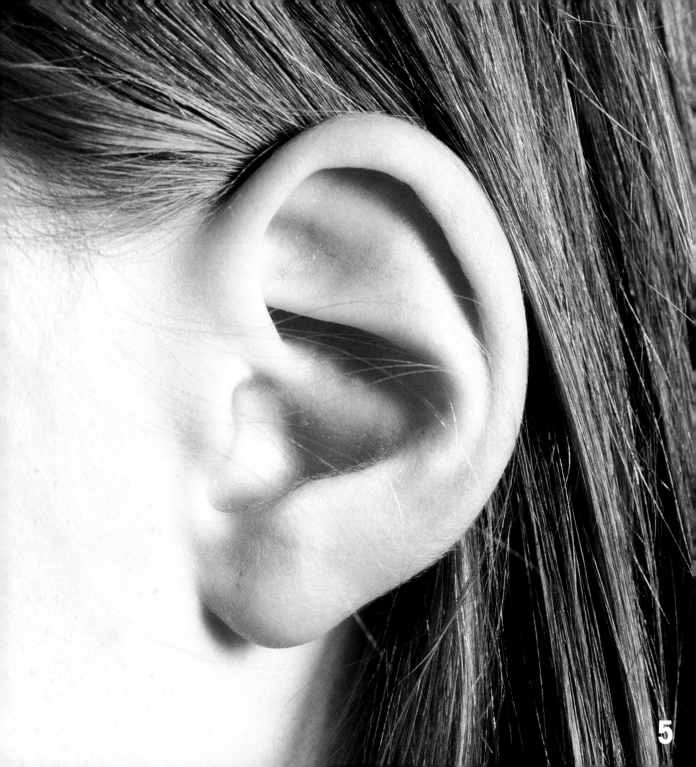

5

In One Ear...

Do your ears rattle when you clap your hands? You cannot feel it, but they do.

Actions, such as speaking or clapping, cause air to shake very quickly. This moving air is called a sound wave.

Sound waves shake the eardrums. The brain can tell how fast they shake. It turns this information into sounds we can hear. It takes only part of a second to do this.

Cover Your Ears!

Why is a cat's meow much quieter than a jet engine? Quiet sounds make small sound waves. Loud sounds have stronger sound waves. They cause large movements in the air. Some sound waves are so strong that they can damage your eardrums.

The loudest sound in history was made in Indonesia in 1883. This was when the Krakatoa volcano **erupted**.

Mood Music

Has music ever made you feel happy or sad? Songs and other sounds can change the way we feel.

Many people feel happy when they listen to songs in a **major key**. The *Star Spangled Banner* is a major key song. **Minor key** music, such as *The Cat Came Back*, can create feelings of sadness.

Loud or sudden sounds, such as a car horn, can scare us. These sounds can be a warning of danger nearby. The sound of someone crying may make you feel sad.

Two Ears Are Better Than One

How do you know where a sound is coming from? The distance between your ears gives your brain clues.

A sound coming from your left reaches your left ear first. It takes longer for the sound to reach your right ear. This is how you know that the sound is coming from your left.

What is an Echo?

What happens when you stamp your feet in a large, empty room? Do you hear the sound more than once?

Sometimes, sound waves bounce back when they hit a solid object. These bounces sound like quiet copies of the first sound. This is called an echo.

It can take sound a long time to bounce back in large spaces. An echo can take more than 10 seconds to bounce back in parts of the Grand Canyon.

Hearing Underwater

Have you ever tried talking to a friend under water? The water muffles the sound.

Whales and dolphins have fatty pouches around their ears. These pouches let them hear clearly under water.

Whales and dolphins use sound to sense their surroundings. They make loud clicking sounds that echo off objects. The echoes let them make a picture of their surroundings.

17

Hearing Over Time

Can you hear all of the notes on a piano? Your parents may not hear some of them as well as you can. As people age, their ears become less **sensitive** to quiet and high-**pitched** sounds.

Children have much sharper hearing than adults. Adults hear much better than seniors.

Try blowing a dog whistle. You cannot hear the sound, but it is very loud to dogs. They can hear much higher-pitched sounds than humans.

Amazing Ears

How do cats balance on narrow logs or land on their feet when they fall? Like people, they have a special set of tubes inside their ears called the labyrinth.

Parts of the labyrinth are filled with fluid. The brain measures how this fluid moves. This tells the brain if you are standing up, lying down, or moving.

Cats have a very sensitive labyrinth. This gives them a very good sense of balance.

Test Your Sense of Hearing

Supplies
A partner, a public street, and a playground

1. Find a street with a little bit of traffic, and stand on the sidewalk.

2. Close your eyes.

3. Listen for the sound of a car moving by.

4. Tell your partner which way you think the car is moving. Do this five times, and then, switch places with your partner. How many did you get right?

1. Go to a playground with a partner. Stand far apart from each other.

2. Close your eyes, and call your partner's name. He or she should call back by saying your name. Keeping your eyes closed, use your sense of hearing to try to find your partner.

3. Have your partner say your name a few times quietly and loudly. Is it easier to find your partner when he or she is speaking quietly or loudly? Can you tell which direction his or her voice is coming from?

4. Switch with your partner, and try again.

Find Out More

To learn more about hearing, visit these websites.

How Stuff Works
http://health.howstuffworks.
com/hearing.htm

ZOOM Science
http://pbskids.org/
zoom/activities/sci/#senses

Your Sense of Hearing
http://library.thinkquest.org/
3750/hear/hear.html

Neuroscience for Kids
www.dls.ym.edu.tw/
chudler/bigear.html

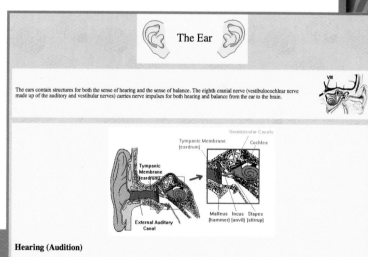

The Ear

The ears contain structures for both the sense of hearing and the sense of balance. The eighth cranial nerve (vestibulocochlear nerve made up of the auditory and vestibular nerves) carries nerve impulses for both hearing and balance from the ear to the brain.

Hearing (Audition)

Sound waves cause the tympanic membrane (eardrum) to vibrate. Humans can hear sounds waves with frequencies between 20 and 20,000 Hz. The three bones in the ear (malleus, incus, stapes) pass these vibrations on to the cochlea. The cochlea is a snail-shaped, fluid-filled structure in the inner ear. Inside the cochlea is another structure called the organ of Corti. Hair cells are located on the basilar membrane of the cochlea. The cilia (the hair) of the hair cells make contact with another membrane called the tectorial membrane. When the hair cells are excited by vibration, a nerve impulse is generated in the auditory nerve. These impulses are then sent to the brain.

(By the way...the stapes is the smallest bone in the human body. It is only 0.25 to 0.33 cm long [0.10 to 0.13 inches] and weighs only 1.9 to 4.3 milligrams.)

Glossary

erupted: exploded with fire and noise

major key: a tune with regular intervals between notes

minor key: a tune with irregular intervals between notes

pitched: how high or low a sound seems

pulses: short bursts

senses: the ways the body gets information about what is happening in its surroundings

sensitive: able to detect

Index